YOUR KNOWLEDGE HAS VALUE

AF141638

- We will publish your bachelor's and master's thesis, essays and papers

- Your own eBook and book - sold worldwide in all relevant shops

- Earn money with each sale

Upload your text at www.GRIN.com and publish for free

Mumtaz Mazumdar

The First English Novel from an African female: "Efuru" by Flora Nwapa

GRIN Verlag

Bibliografische Information der Deutschen Nationalbibliothek:

Die Deutsche Bibliothek verzeichnet diese Publikation in der Deutschen National-
bibliografie; detaillierte bibliografische Daten sind im Internet über http://dnb.d-
nb.de/ abrufbar.

Imprint:

Copyright © 2013 GRIN Verlag GmbH
Druck und Bindung: Books on Demand GmbH, Norderstedt Germany
ISBN: 978-3-656-37623-1

This book at GRIN:

http://www.grin.com/en/e-book/209666/the-first-english-novel-from-an-african-
female-efuru-by-flora-nwapa

GRIN - Your knowledge has value

Der GRIN Verlag publiziert seit 1998 wissenschaftliche Arbeiten von Studenten, Hochschullehrern und anderen Akademikern als eBook und gedrucktes Buch. Die Verlagswebsite www.grin.com ist die ideale Plattform zur Veröffentlichung von Hausarbeiten, Abschlussarbeiten, wissenschaftlichen Aufsätzen, Dissertationen und Fachbüchern.

Visit us on the internet:

http://www.grin.com/

http://www.facebook.com/grincom

http://www.twitter.com/grin_com

Introduction

Nigeria one of the nations in West Africa is at present in the global news for violent clashes among religious groups. Like the other African states, it too is basically a multi-ethnic nation. The Igbos are one of the four major Nigerian tribes along with the Hausas, the Fulanis along with the Yorubas. (1) The Igbos consist of seventeen percent of the Nigerians living in the South-eastern region. Keeping a historical record of the Igbos of the past, have been done in the traditional oral songs and proverbs. This is perhaps the very ancient literary practice. The written African records are the pictograph forms. Egypt is considered the oldest African example of pictographs. If the pictographs echoed the 'indigenity' (2) of the ethnic tribes of Africa, so did the oral tradition of Nigeria. The Igbos showed its 'indigenity' via its songs and proverbs. These songs which have been transmitted from generation to generation were mostly sung by the women. And they mostly consisted about the lives of the male heroes. The oral traditions remain forever. A Ghanaian proverb says,

Ancient things remain in the ear. (3)

The oral practice still remains in speech and writing. And the first writing script in Nigeria along with the many North and Western African states was Arabic. The Christian missionaries, who arrived later, have been most successful with the Igbos in making them change to Roman script. (4) Male writers have been dominant before and at the eve of the Independence in 1960. These writers penned books with men as the protagonists. It is stunning and ironical that they found nothing to write about women although women form half of the humanity in any nation. Women's presences in the making of the collective whole were left behind by the shortsighted writers. For example, there was the presence of domestic slavery of women within Nigeria before trans-Atlantic slave trade or before the entry of the British colonizers. Later, women were sold under 'legitimate' items along with other products in the Bights of Benin and Biafra as part of the same slave trade. This was most possible in the Southeastern Nigeria. Half of those slaves were young African girls and children. The male writers rarely confessed about these historic trades. Eras of Igbo domination arrived and disappeared. Their leader Ojukwu agitated to secede as Biafra. In this post-Independence movement the Igbo women paid tremendous role. But such female participation remained unexposed by male writers. Leaving aside these slave trades and war-deeds by the women, there are deeper roles of Igbo women in the society. Igbo women have been forever webbed in the economic, family and religious world of the Igbo ethnic society. But these too have not been completely covered by any writer until Flora Nwapa with her debut novel *Efuru*, in the sixth year after Independence. Nwapa was born in 1931 in Oguta in Nigeria. She started her career as a writer with the publication of *Efuru. Idu, Never Again* and *Women are Important* are her later other chief novels. Nwapa remained as an educator teaching at colleges and universities around the globe, throughout her life. She died in 1993.

Efuru was written when the world has already finished facing the Great Wars of mass destruction and history of genocide. Then followed the 1940s and the 60s of the emergence of post-colonial nations most of which were liberated from the British including Nigeria. The new cultural colonizer that is, the United States of America in another continent was going through the impacts of the Harlem to gather the pride of being blacks. The cry of Pan-Africanism was echoing to emotionally and culturally unite the dispersed blacks of the world. There were also the making of their presences felt by the Diasporic blacks in various write-ups. All these topics and the famous Middle Passage or the Biafran Civil War has also nothing to do in Nwapa's *Efuru*. Oils and petroleum revenues were the latest economic knowledge available to young Nigerian men. Nwapa seeped into core issues related to ever dominant *episteme* of the social life of an ordinary Igbo peasant woman. The book is named after the protagonist Efuru. Efuru is shown as an independent woman who fails in both her marriages due to childlessness. In a country where Igbos were fast getting introduced to a world religion named Christianity, Efuru finds relief in her ancient Igbo religion. She finds space in being a selected worshipper of one of the Igbo Goddesses or Mami Wata.

The Igbo Earning Woman

Despite her economic independence Efuru failed to linger her social position in relation to marriage and family. Being an earner as female is as old as the ethnics. African women have been involved beyond cooking, household chores or decking up home premises. Economy connected Efuru to her marriages and family. Family lies at the center of social and economic fabric of society. It is for the making of these families that led the majority Igbo people from ancient times to become farmers, cattle herders and hunters. Igbo women have always been contributing at par with their men in the economic progress of their respective families. Actually, there have been not much rigid and clear divisions of profession between men and women. Women took part in farming along with the men. There is the instance of the Tonga plateau in Southern Zambia. Hoe is usually taken to be the weapon of the female worker in the field. (5)

The traits of farming continue even today in African societies. And Efuru is one of these African peasant women whose life is shown in the novel. Flora Nwapa has taken up the most common Igbo woman. The condition of the peasant woman was declining during the colonial rule. The introduction of the new cash crops by the British regime like, peanuts, cotton, cocoa and coffee were changing the economic organizations of the rural world. Men became interested in these as this brought faster money. The women kept on struggling with the old types of cultivation. Colonization brought another wrap of gender-divided tasks. Trades were always gendered over the globe, including Nigeria. This example of the cassava and the yam is one. After experience with the whites, Yam and cassava now remained exclusively to the Igbo women. Before the advent of the whites, cassava was cultivated by the Igbo female and yams by the males. Nigerian agriculture has always been based on yam. And it is still part of all basic rituals and festivals of the Igbos. The Igbo women took more control over its production now. There is a very unique thing to notice here. It is that women have always been able to accept and pass all tests given to her, including this switch over in cultivation. She could show more flexibility. It coincides with Julia Kristeva's description of the flexible and the 'unifying' nature of the female language, which she calls 'semiotic.' (6) Efuru too could do so. When she married Adizua, the success with income depended more upon her hard work. Adizua was laughed at by his fellow farmers for being unable to make profit. But his wife consoled and encouraged him to wait and work for the better. She directed him to first try trade in yams, dry fish and crayfish. Crayfish brought full fortune to them. Adizua's mother was so delighted with her daughter-in-law that she openly confessed to Efuru's father Nwashike Ogene,

Your daughter has brought luck into our family. (7)

Nwashike Ogene, your daughter is the best of women. (8)

She exerted more power in this economic process. As per the terms of Michel Foucault, Efuru becomes the *machinery of alliance* (9) in this marriage system. And this marriage alliance later diminishes and ultimately ends giving way to Efuru's incomplete motherhood. The sexuality takes over the economic alliance in marriage. This transfer is described as,

What we are witnessing is what Foucault calls the 'entry of life into history,' (10)

It can be seen how the ordinary life of a rural woman is as historical as the lives of the bourgeoisie. The importance of the biological phenomenon takes over economic alliances. And the ability of Flora Nwapa's portrayal of such changes is a very modern attempt in her narrative. The plot is traditional and contemporary too.

The quotes from the novel also show how women could be motivators to men. They can change the man's destiny. It can be observed that the sense of success of the family can be deeper in women in such cases. The determination to earn and run the family well is seen in Efuru. The reason to such action can be traced back to past. Men in Africa have been travelers and hunters from time immemorial. In their absences, women have been covering the economic needs of the homes. So earning or participating in livelihood does not scare the African woman. Nor does she sulk about it. As a result, they have not been stereotypes. Nwapa apprehended these historical aspects and created a dynamic woman in Efuru too. The African female therefore is naturally expected to earn and add to the economy of the father's or the husband's family. Such expectations were known to Western culture. The concept of the practice of the bride price among the Igbos is said to have come from this economical drive. The groom's family is to pay bride price in 'cash' to the bride's family because he is robbing an asset from them by taking her away. But this concept to earn can become meaningless after marriage, as in the case of Efuru if the woman is unable to bear children. The woman is actually shown as helpless and scapegoat in all kinds of social institutions.

The Igbo Marriage

Abandoning wife is originally unknown among the Igbo marital rules. But Adizua did it. So this was double-standards practiced by Igbo husbands. It is also very ironical that Adizua once sworn that he can never exchange Efuru with a wife would give him twenty sons. But the same Adizua came out to be a fake lover of wife. It can also be noted that these kind of male representation was absent by the prominent male writers earlier. Efuru's easy compliance to Azidua's intimacy with another woman may stun readers of other parts of the globe. The narrative of *Efuru* had started taking turning point when Adizua had to go outside the village for job and livelihood. He gets involved in the company of another woman. Efuru knew about it. Plural marriages by men were not unknown to the Igbo world. She was not objecting to his marrying a second wife. Rather she said,

I do not object to being relegated to the background. I want to keep my position as the first wife, for it is my right. (11)

The confession of Efuru reveals striking truths about her marriage. Efuru remembers how Adizua had changed with time and how he treated her,

. ...the way that only slaves are treated. God in heaven will judge us. (12)

But Nwapa is determined to continue her dynamic woman in Efuru. Nwapa puts the following dialogue in the mouth of Efuru,

If Adizua does not love me any more, I too will try to learn not to love him any more. It will be a difficult task but it not impossible. (13)

The further story reveals from the mouth of Efuru's mother-in-law how Adizua's father too had acted similar to Efuru's mother-in-law as what Adizua was now doing to Efuru. She was helped by her sister Ajanupu and their mother to begin a small trade in fish to grow up Adizua. When her husband returned, he was already full of diseases. This parallel story or memory of her mother-in-law's past in the otherwise chronological narrative is also a striking rare *episteme* made available to the readers. Earning to live for oneself or other family members was not scaring to Efuru or her mother-in-law. Nwapa discovers the various aspects of the live s of the Igbo woman. When Adizua left Efuru as his father did to his mother in the past, she too soon started keeping herself engaged in micro-enterprises. In the 1960s women have outnumbered males in the agricultural area. Male peasants had become much fewer in comparison to the females. There were coming up new women farmers. There were becoming businesswomen and entrepreneurs too. However, some like Efuru worked in the home fields without much remuneration. What offered was almost insignificant. Efuru coincides in all these historical perspectives. But it was a natural social institution. The evidence can be found in the pre-colonial setting of *The Rape of Shavi* written by Flora Nwapa's follower Igbo writer in English named Buchi Emecheta. In this novel of the Igbo world, we find the Chief marrying another young woman. The perfect villages of Shavi were distracted by the holocaust of the plane Newark, which consisted of the whites transgressed the dignity of the would-be female queen of Shavi. The would-be father-in-law would was the Chief. And he practiced polygamy as a usual thing. The Chief Queen Shoshovi's anguish was known to the husband and so clearly brought out to the readers too. But it is seen that the Chief did not feel the necessity to correct himself and stop polygamy. Rather, he was enjoying Shoshovi's dance which she did as reaction in anguish and helplessness to give release to her pent-up feelings against the going-to-be marriage of her husband. The studying of these thoughtful inner readings of the minds of Efuru and Shoshovi are very subjective and modern elements in the literature of Nigeria. So it can be understood that did the Igbo female and wife really accept the polygamous nature of the males in the traditional societies but never abandon any wife. In *Efuru* failure of motherhood gives Efuru's husband chance to avail the same custom. Nwapa shows that even a pure traditional society could be porous with drawbacks for the Igbo female. The role of marriage is most important in the life of a woman. A woman is glorified in reproduction of the male child. Marriage and motherhood go together for them. A daughter was born to Efuru. But it was a short-lived motherhood. Ojonim died in early childhood. Even the prayers to the ancestors failed to save Ojonim. And the absence of children changes Efuru's destiny. What Adizua did, Glibert attempted something more. Efuru's second marriage to Gilbert was becoming stagnant too because she failed to have any children. The motive of marriage is to beget children from the wife. The expectations of the relatives, neighbours and the friends too seem the same. Adizua's family thought why he should not marry another woman since according to them; two men do not live together. To them Efuru was a man since she could not reproduce. The society which consisted of kins and neighbours had made life miserable for Efuru. Nnona says to her,

It is true that a person who has people is better off than a person who has money. (14)

The other Igbo women commented upon Efuru and Gilbert that happy marriages without children cannot be eaten and said,

Of what use is it if it is not fruitful. Of what is it if husbands licks your body, worships you and buys everything in the market for you and you are not productive? (15)

These women choked the fire more. Again some women like Ajanupu were different and thoughtful who wanted to help Efuru. Ajanupu kept on explaining to Efuru that the latter should let others know that Efuru wanted her husband to marry another woman and have children. If she left it to Gilbert and the mother-in-law, then they may get someone who might override her. Efuru will have no control over the co-wife and this would become difficult for Efuru. This may lead Gilbert and his second wife any day shows Efuru the exit door of the house for being childless. Ajanupu's advice transformed Efuru's heart to unending sadness.

After her second marriage to Gilbert, Efuru had once fallen ill. The dibias or male Igbo soothsayers alleged her adulterous. They said that the sicknesses arrived because she was ill-charactered. Her age-group women of the community accompanied Efuru to the temple of Utuosa to witness her prayers and let her get killed by the God if she was really adulterous. No Gods killed Efuru. But it is ironical that her first husband Adizua was never questioned about his character when he returned back home. It can be observed that the Patriarchy is never questioned in both these marriages. Patriarchy remains constant. It is nearly non-colonial setting, yet critics like Betty Friedan, Kate Millett and Shulamith Firestone showed reminded that patriarchy were one of the few powerful elements which were at the root of all evils in society. (16) Nwapa has too shown this successfully. Rather, she takes up the tool of writing by rather showing the female movements. She reexamines the Igbo society from the first stage of traditional presence. She systematically calls from the beginning and draws no rosy picture of the traditional Igbo society and customs in their female treatment of the Igbo female. The multi-structured layers of oppression of the Igbo Efuru are brought here. Efuru represented the drawbacks of pure Igbo society in their dealings with women. Nwapa shows that even a pure traditional society could be porous with drawbacks for the Igbo female. The role of marriage is most important in the life of an Igbo woman. An Igbo woman is glorified in reproduction of the male child.

The Igbo Religion

Childlessness was changing Efuru's fate. The role of the ancestors and the deities are inevitable in the lives of the Igbos. Earlier in her first marriage to Adizua, Efuru provoked the ancestors to save her daughter. The role of ancestors in the code of religious practices is severe in the Igbo world. Ancestors are so important that one wishes to die, go and rest with one's ancestors. The ancestors were expected to bless Efuru with baby. She was consoled that the ancestors will not allow her to remain barren. Later, when her daughter Ojonim fell ill, Efuru invokes the ancestors to save her daughter. She provokes,

Our ancestors fight against death, don't let death defeat you. (17)

But it is an irony that the ancestors who had earlier somehow blessed her with a daughter snatched her few years old daughter away from her. Later, as her second husband Gilbert was almost getting ready to marry again, Efuru was slowly turning to one of the Igbo Goddesses or Mami Wata named Uhamiri. Uhamiri is in truth Goddess of wealth. She was not the Goddess to give the wealth of children to any woman. It is ironical that Efuru seeks goes to such Mami Wata. She goes to the lake Goddess Uhamiri to bless her with children. But she remains unrewarded. Nigeria was going through the experience of Christianity. But the Igbo religion still remains at parallel. The religion carries tribal essence. The local deities have always been so important from the pre-colonial times. The female Goddesses have been very important from time immemorial for the Igbos. These deities attracted clients from faraway places too. That is sometimes they exerted influence beyond the Igbos. These trans-local deities are considered highly powerful. In fact they held sometimes held central positions in the lives of the Igbos. In Flora Nwapa's Efuru's case, an early female deity played major role in her life. It was religion which ultimately stabled Efuru's life. The Igbo mythical religion prevailed there yet. But Nwapa takes no backseat in making them represent themselves. There is the local belief system and social environment in Efuru. The days of pre-colonial might be over. But the effects and practices of traditional religions of the Igbos still persist. Nwapa creates an ideal world of the mythical religion of the Igbos. The mythical Goddess comes to Efuru's rescue. Efuru even sees dreams which unite Efuru with Uhamiri. She relates her dreams to her excited father,

I dream several nights of the lake and the woman of the lake. Two nights ago, the dream was very vivid. I was swimming in the lake, when a fish raised its head and asked me to follow it. Foolishly I swam out to follow it. It dived and I dived too. I got to the bottom of the lake and to my surprise, I saw an elegant woman, very beautiful, combing her long black hair with a golden comb. When she saw me, she stopped combing her hair and smiled at me and asked me to come in. (18)

Efuru therefore considers herself selected worshipper of Uhamiri. This ethnic religion has been handed down via oral songs. Efuru is reminded of one of the pathetic songs she used to hear from one of the woman.

Uhamiri Please / Uhamiri Please / Uhamiri the goddess, please / Uhamiri the thunder, please / Uhamiri the Kind, please / Uhamiri the beautiful, please (19)

Nwapa makes tribal societies look full and superior to the urban civilization. In practice, many consider tribal religions as always inferior. But Nwapa takes the readers quite deeper into the matter and rethink upon these constructed conceptions. In fact, Nwapa shows the importance of the Mami Wata in the first chapter itself. Efuru was here considered so beautiful that one would think that the woman of the lake was her mother. She was in fact, compared to the Mami Wata, Uhamiri and was chosen very ironical about what the belief about the female protagonist was. The Nnobi or the Nigerian Igbo believed in a myth that the first married a Goddess, Idemili who demanded that she and her daughter Edo be worshipped all over the land, although later on she is found domesticated by the males. Women and religion get closely related to each other in African societies. Female figures have been worshipped by men from a long time in many societies all over the world. So it is the same in the Nigerian societies. Women are also considered the healers, as Goddess Uhamiri comes to heal Efuru. A woman is powerless if she fails to acquire motherhood. This powerlessness makes her an outcaste. The Igbo society's reality failed to console and give space to Efuru. But the mythical Uhamiri empowers Efuru.

Conclusion

Women found new voice in art forms. Flora Nwapa led the group in Nigeria. Literature became the most profound tool in the international arena for the Igbo writers who are females. And their being educated added to their availing the medium of expression in novels too. Some French male and female writers had once attempted to show the sad states of the black females in the past before Nwapa's attempt. But surely this was not enough. Some had been attempting English too. However Nigerian Nwapa began best. Nwapa intertwines the old and the new in expression. She takes aid of the ancient oral literature to represent the ancient world of the Igbos. She makes the audible Igbo ancient in the written form. At the same time Nwapa delves in the modern subjective elements of the characters, particularly of the female protagonist Efuru. Nwapa also shows tremendous influence in the theme of motherhood. Men and women have to begin their lives from the naval of the mothers. But this sublime institution went unnoticed until it caught Nwapa's attention. Chinua Achebe reiterated *mother is supreme*. (20) But this line was not really enough. It is Nwapa who delved into the deepest perspectives of motherhood. Male writers defined to disappointed love. They forgot the perspectives of polygamy and marriage even. Rather these latter two institutions are only related to disappointed love. Nwapa talks of the social inferiority of women. She shows the market economy in relation to Efuru's personal life. She shows the role of religion and myths in relation to Efuru's marriage and personal happiness. She shows how a woman's whole life may take place within marriage and motherhood only. Another thing is that women especially in the countryside still need help in decision makings. She should be taught about the importance and availability of free thinking and education. She should be thought to dream and design for herself for future. Even Flora Nwapa's heroine is shown as a decision-maker.

End Notes

1. Yoruba women in Nigeria are said to be famous for being great weavers. They embroidered a kind of cloth called *bazin*. Unlike Ghana's case Nigerian women who had no connection with the European trade world did made their own nexus. Women formed their own market associations. They were underestimated by the colonials for being illiterates. Igbo women were food traders basically. For useful secondary literature see Harneit-Sievers Axel's *Constructions of Belonging Igbo Communities and the Nigerian State in the Twentieth Century*. Yoruba women's being weavers proves about the ethnic women's involvement in the economic aspects of lives.

2. "Indigenity" is elaborately defined in Axel Harneit-Sievers's book *Constructions of Belonging Igbo Communities and the Nigerian State in the Twentieth Century* in the Introduction pages in 1 and 2

3. See in page xi of Jan Vansina's Oral Tradition as History.

4. See Harneit-Siever's Introduction Pages.

5. See Pages 11-12 of Catherine Coquery-Vidrovitch's *African Women*, A Modern History.

6. See Page 159 of Ross Murfin and Supriya M. Ray *The Bedford Glossary of Critical and Literary Terms*.

7. See page 187 of Alan Sinfield's *Michel Foucault:The Will to Truth*.

8. See Page 22 of *Efuru*.

9. See Page 23 of *Efuru*.

10. In Alan Sinfield's Page 191.

11. See Page 53 of *Efuru*.

12. See Page 58 of *Efuru*.

13. See Page 58 of *Efuru.*

14. See Page 131 of Efuru.

15. See Page 137 of Efuru.

16. See Page 5 of Elizabeth Wright's Postmodern Encounters, *Lacan and Postfeminism.*

17. See Page 67 of *Efuru.*

18. See Page 146 of *Efuru.*

19. See Page 147 of *Efuru.*

20. See, Ato Quayson Ato and Tejumola Olaniyan's *African Literature. An Anthology of Criticism and Theory.*

Works Cited

1. Catherine Kroll "Domestic Disturbances: African Women's Cultural Production in the Postcolonial Continuum" Research in African Literatures 41.3;136-146; Fall 2010.

2. Rhonda Wells-Wilbon and Gaynell Marie Simpson "Transitioning the Caregiving Role for the Next Generation: An African-Centered Womanist Perspective" Black Women, Gender & Families 3.2; 87-105; Fall 2009.

3. F. Abiola Irele, editor *The Cambridge Companion to the African novel* UK Cambridge UP; 2009

4. Toyin Falola and Mathew M. Heaton *History of Nigeria* UK Cambridge UP; 2008

5. Savage Barbara Dianne *Your Spirits Walk Beside Us The Politics of Black Religion* Massachusetts The Belknap Press of Harvard University Press Massachusetts; 2008

6. Kyungwon Hong Grace "The Future of Our Worlds": Black Feminism and the Politics of Knowledge in the University under Globalization" Meridians: feminism, race, transnationalism 8.2; 95-115; 2008

7. Ato Quayson and Olaniyan Tejumola, editors *African Literature An Anthology of Criticism and Theory* Oxford Blackwell Publishing; 2007

8. Caroline Rooney *Decolonising Gender Literature and the Poetics of the Real* London and New York Routledge; 2007

9. Udeani Chibueze *Inculturation as Dialogue Igbo Culture and the Message of Christ* Amsterdam-New York Rodopi; 2007

10.Yaw Oheneba-Saki and Baffour K. Takyi ,editors *African Families at the turn of the 21st century* OUP, London;2006.

11. Axel Harneit-Sievers *Constructions of Belonging Igbo Communities and the Nigerian State in the Twentieth Century* USA University of Rochester Press; 2006.

21. Gale Thompson *Feminism in Literature Vol 5:20th* USA *Century Authors*;2005

22. Alain Ricard and Flora Veit-Wild, editors *Interfaces Between the Oral and the Written Versions and Subversions in African Literatures 2* Amsterdam-New York Rodopi;2005

14. Nnaemeka Obioma ,editor *The Politics of (M)Othering Womanhood, identity, and resistance in African literature* London and New York Routledge;2005

15. Zeleza Tiyambe "The Politics and Poetics of Exile: Edward Said in Africa" Research in African Literatures 36.3;1-22; Fall 2005

16. Iris Berger "Feminism, Patriarchy, and African Women's History" Journal of Women's History 20.2; 130-135; Summer 2005

17. Simon Gikandi *Encyclopedia of African Literature* Routledge London and New York;2005.

18. Buchi Emecheta *The wrestling Match* New York George Braziller; 2005

19. Kinser Amber E "Negotiating Spaces For/Through Third-Wave Feminism" NWSA Journal 16.3; 124-153; Fall 2004

20. R. Victoria Arana and Lauri Ramey *Black British Writing* New York Palgrave Macmillan; 2004.

21. Sandhu Sukhdev *London Calling: How Black and Asian Writers Imagined a City* London Harper Perennial; 2004.

22. Alphen Ernst van, editor *Africa and Its Significant Others Thamyris Intersecting: Place, Sex, and Race* New York Rodopi; 2003

23. Ross Murfin and Supriya M. Ray *The Bedford Glossary of Critical and Literary Terms* London Palgrave Macmillan; 2003

24. Erwin Lee "Genre and Authority in Some Popular Nigerian Women's Novels" <u>Research in African Literatures</u> 33.2; 81-99; Summer 2002

25. Amadiume Ifi "Bodies, Choices, Globalizing Neocolonial Enchantments: African Matriarchs and Mammy Wata" <u>Meridians: feminism, race, transnationalism</u> 2.2; 41-66; 2002

26. Carolyn Kumat *African women and literature* West African Review: vol.2, No1; 2002

27. Elizabeth Wright *Postmodern Encounters Lacan and Postfeminism* D. K. Fine Art Press (P) Ltd. Delhi, 2001

28. Catherine Coquery-Vidrovitch editor *African Women A Modern History,* Social Change in Global Perspective Colorado West Press View; 1997

29. Adebayo Diran *Some Kind of Black* London Virago; 1996

30. Alan Sinfield *Michel Foucault A Will to Truth* Routledge London 1990

31. Catherine Obianuju Acholonu *Western and Indigenous Traditions in Modern Igbo Literature* Research in African Literatures: Vol. 20, No.1; Spring 1989

32. Shabnam Grewal, editor *Charting the Journey. Writings by Black and Third World Women* London Sheba Feminist Publishers;1989

33. Nancy Topping Bazin *Feminist Perspectives in African Fiction: Bessie Head and Buchi Emecheta* Black Scholar, 17.2 (1986)

34. Jan Vansina *Oral Tradition as History* The University of Wisconsin Press, USA; 1985

35. Nancy Topping Bazin "Weight of customs, Signs of Change: Feminism in the Literature of African Women," World Literature Written in English, volume 25, No 2; 183-197; 1983

36. Buchi Emecheta *The Rape of Shavi* London Ogwugwu Afo; 1983

37. Buchi Emecheta *The Joys of Motherhood* Oxford Heinemann; 1980

38. Adrienne Rich *Of Women Born: Motherhood as Experience and Institution* New York: Bantam 20; 1997

39. Prema Nandakumar "An Image of African Womanhood (A Study of Flora Nwapa's Efuru)," African Quarterly, 11, No.2; 136-46; 1971

40. Flora Nwapa *Idu* Oxford Heinemann;1970

41. Flora Nwapa *Efuru* Oxford Heinemann. Oxford; 1966